A SPIRIT DAUGHTER WORKBOOK

WRITTEN BY
JILL WINTERSTEEN

FOR THE FULL MOON

MONDAY, JANUARY 17TH, 2022
3:48 PM PT

THE FULL MOON

The Full Moon is the height of the lunar cycle. It marks the midway point from one New Moon to another and signifies a time of revelation. We plant intentions on the New Moon through creative visions and intuitive awakening. The Full Moon is when we see what we must break through, process, and release in order to manifest those intentions. It's a time to embody the changes we desire in our lives and begin to see ourselves in a new light—the light of the Full Moon.

The Full Moon often feels emotionally intense to our systems. It brings up energy and emotions that we can comfortably avoid at other times. On a Full Moon, though, everything is brought to light and we see ourselves in our full totality. This all-encompassing view shows us our higher vibrations, which help us manifest our intentions, and our lower vibrations, which work to sabotage our greatest efforts. We can see the full range of energy, emotions, behaviors, and reactions on a Full Moon. This revelation can feel overwhelming at first, but when we face ourselves courageously, what we once feared no longer has power over us.

As the Moon faces the Sun, we are working with the power of day and night, light and shadows, along with the seen and the unseen. We have the opportunity to expose and understand unconscious patterns that govern us. We are also working with opposing zodiac signs where the Moon and Sun are positioned. These energies are activated in our consciousness, and we can clearly see them in our energy. We can become aware of how we align with certain zodiac qualities on a Full Moon. No matter our personal Sun or Moon sign, we all have the twelve energies of the zodiac within our energetic fields. They are archetypal patterns that are universal to all beings. Even if you are a Leo or a Pisces, you still hold the energy of Cancer and Capricorn in your field and align with these energies in some way.

Over a Full Moon, you can clearly see if you are aligning with the higher or lower vibrations of a zodiac sign. Every energy, including astrological energies, has a high side and a low side. The energies work together to create a full spectrum of frequencies governed by an astrological sign. On a Full Moon, we have the chance to understand these frequencies and acknowledge how they might manifest in emotions, personalities, behaviors, and energy. We can become aware if these vibrations make up a shadow side, which is just out of our view but still powerful in controlling us. We can also see which energies serve as our greatest assets and need nourishment.

When you do identify a lower vibration in your field, it's important to first accept it and know there is nothing inherently wrong, or even personal about it. These energies are universal to everyone. It is not just you who experiences them. They show up in many forms in other beings. The first step in working with your lower frequencies is to acknowledge how you feel about them. Notice if guilt, shame, resentment, or denial surfaces. Honor these emotions and know that these lower vibrations are simply part of being alive. They are simply patterns of energy. You are not the only one who feels this way, nor are you the only person to align with these lower energies.

Once you've accepted places in your life where these lower vibrations show up, know that you can shift them to higher ones. The Full Moon brings an opportunity each month to not only release energies, but to transmute them into new vibrations. Through awareness and intention, we can change these energies and channel them into something else. They can become places of power, not simply something to get rid of or ignore. All the energy we hold contains power of some kind. It all can be harnessed to create the life of our highest visions. We must be willing to see it in its totality, understand it, accept it, and do the work needed to shift it. The Full Moon is the perfect time to walk the path of turning your shadows into light.

CANCER FULL MOON

The first Full Moon of 2022 falls in the powerful sign of Cancer. Ruled by the Moon herself, Cancer guides us in uncovering our emotions, processing them, and finding our intuition. This Moon is always an emotionally intense time when we are asked to have patience with ourselves as we soften and acknowledge what lies beneath our exteriors.

As a cardinal Water sign, Cancer helps us generate the power of water within ourselves. Water helps us heal, connect with our spirits, and replenish our souls. It reminds us that we are both soft and fierce. It also teaches us the magic of slow change. Just as the ocean gently molds the shoreline, we too can shape our lives how we desire if we are willing to be patient. There will be times when we need to move slowly and softly, and there will be times when we need to roar and crash. Both of these sides are beautiful and necessary for carving out our place in this world.

Water is also the original home of all life and helps us come home to ourselves. It teaches us what feels good to the soul and what helps us feel settled, protected, and at ease in our bodies. Whether it's the sound of the sea or syncing our breath with the waves, the ocean brings us back to a time we were held in her softness and protected from the other elements of life. When working with the power of water, we are connecting with our home frequency—the vibration that allows us to feel centered, held, and immensely powerful. This Full Moon helps us connect to water, the Ocean, and the energies that bring us home.

As you work with the energy of this Full Moon, first acknowledge what helps you feel safe and supported. What lets you know you are safe to feel, shift, and melt your exterior walls?

CANCER FULL MOON

Cancer is represented by the crab, who uses its hard shell to contain its emotions and keep them close to its heart. Life is not about staying hidden, though. It's about growth—especially growth through vulnerability. Even the crab must leave the safety of its old shell in order to grow into a new one. In the space between homes, the crab is exposed to elements that force it to rely on instinct and intuition alone. Just as the crab evolves through times of transition, so do you, even if they make your feel vulnerable or afraid. The silver lining of uncertainty is that it gives you no choice but to trust your inner knowledge and power.

Over this Full Moon, feel if you need to leave your old shell full of patterns of safety and limitations for a new shell, capable of holding your expansive self. Is a fear of the unknown holding you back from taking a leap of faith or allowing yourself to grow? Know the journey from one shell to another can feel intense and even vulnerable, but when you trust your intuition, the path becomes less challenging. Feel into what transformation is calling to you this Full Moon. Allow yourself to process all the emotions it brings so you take the steps you need to evolve this next year.

This Full Moon heightens your intuition along with your emotions. Cancer teaches that the two go hand in hand. You cannot access your inner wisdom without feeling your way there. If you shut yourself off from feeling or suppress your emotions, your intuition is also lost. While this Moon may bring up some tears and emotional outbursts, it will also give you great insights into what steps you need to take on your journey. It will bring forth inner knowledge that you know with your entire being is correct for you right now. It brings out your magic.

Give yourself space to feel this Full Moon. Acknowledge what gives you support. Then, with that support, sit with your feelings. Have a conversation with them and learn from them. Your emotions hold potent information. They can tell you what holds you back from your visions, what you need to reprocess to move forward, and how you can accept life as it occurs. Your emotions contain energy that can be channeled into creating the life you want. Feel into them this Full Moon and honor them. Honor your waves and the fluctuating Water element within you.

Once you've felt your emotions, feel what knowledge they are giving you. After having felt your heart, what do you understand about yourself? What do you now know about your life and your journey? Intuition comes in flashes of brilliance. It cannot be thought out of you. It comes through signs, messages, and even dreams. It feels like an inner knowing. It feels like home. When you feel your intuition, you know it. Your whole body knows it, and it's up to you to follow it. When you do not follow your intuition, it feels like an act of self-betrayal. Honor yourself this Full Moon and honor your wisdom.

As you feel your emotions and intuition, honor how you want to feel. We all have a home frequency that becomes the baseline for how we feel each day. It is the place we return to when the waves of change come upon us. It's our natural state and can recenter our energy, life, and interactions with others. Your home frequency can be one of love, gratitude, peace, contentment, or whatever frequency you want to feel each day. Create ways you return to this frequency no matter what occurs in your life. What will bring you back home to yourself and your intuition? Cultivate this frequency each day, and think of it as your shell. It protects you from the elements of life and creates a container for your emotions. When you need to shift it into a new shell, you can do that too. For now, though, create this vibration within yourself and find ways to maintain it. Allow it to hold you, support you, and give you a place to return to after you've traveled to new frequencies that might have taught you but do not feel like home. Decide how you want to feel this Full Moon, and commit to feeling that way each day as you flow with the waves of life.

CANCER MOON X CAPRICORN SUN

As the Moon lands in Cancer, the Sun lands directly opposite in Capricorn this Full Moon. We have the opportunity to work with both of these energies this day and shift them in our energetic bodies. Capricorn provides a container in which we work with the emotional waters stirred by Cancer. As a cardinal Earth sign, Capricorn generates Earth energy. It helps ground our vibration and creates a feeling of stability as we ride the waves of this Full Moon.

Capricorn and Cancer share many similarities that are illuminated by this Moon. They both help us form creative expressions of our inner worlds so that others can understand us. They both encourage us to spend time alone, honor our intuition, and listen to our inner guidance. They also both ask us to define how we want to feel and create a life that supports those feelings. With the combination of these signs, this Full Moon is deeply introspective and provides insights to emotional wisdom that is otherwise unavailable.

As you journey through this Full Moon, lean into the energy of Capricorn to feel supported by the Earth element. Feel the focus and clarity this energy provides and harness it to understand your emotions and your power. Feel the soft container it provides for you to explore your depths. Capricorn teaches us to honor what is really worth our energy. Feel into what emotions are worth your attention this Full Moon and which ones can teach you the most about yourself.

Over this Full Moon, we can harness the higher sides of both Capricorn and Cancer to help us nourish ourselves and our home frequency for the coming year. We can also see clearly how we may align with the lower frequencies of these signs. In its highest form Cancer teaches us to hold space for our emotions and allow them to show us our intuition. When we align with this side, we give ourselves support to feel and connect with the element of Water within us. We also find our way home to ourselves, where our intuition is the loudest and where we can cultivate any feeling we wish to experience.

The lower vibrations of Cancer occur when suppress our feelings or do not give them the attention they deserve. In this state, we distract ourselves with various methods that allow us to focus on anything but our emotions. We simply do not give ourselves permission to feel. Allow this may feel good in the moment, it does create long lasting positive vibrations. When we ignore our feelings, they manifest in ways we cannot control. They show up as different forms of illnesses, uncontrolled anxiety, and feelings of instability. We need to feel and when we do not give ourselves what we need, our feelings make themselves known in ways we cannot hide from.

If you find yourself aligning with this side of Cancer, give yourself permission to feel. Sit down with yourself and write the sentence, "I feel ..." then allow yourself to write unrestrained. Be open to anything that comes up. If you need to cry, cry. If you need to scream, scream. There is no wrong way to feel, and all of your emotions are valid. No emotion is wrong, and you can feel anything you want. Through this

CANCER MOON X CAPRICORN SUN

allowance, you can ensure that your emotions don't spill over into areas where they don't belong. The other lower vibration of Cancer occurs when emotions not tended to begin to interfere with other areas of your life. This lower side can look like oversharing to unsupportive people, overreacting emotionally in a professional situation, or depending on partners to process emotions for you.

If you find yourself sharing your emotions too often in spaces where it isn't appropriate, take responsibility for them. Know that your emotions do not belong to anyone else and it's ultimately up to you to process them and understand them. Through this awareness, you can gain their wisdom and open the doorway to your intuition. Emotions left unfelt or placed on others can cause disruptions and prevent you from growing. Notice if you are aligning with any of these lower sides of Cancer, and first know that it's ok. Accept that this energy is a part of you right now and that you can shift it. Sit with yourself, explore your emotions, and nourish your heart. Be your own great mother and gently hold yourself as you soften, flow, and find your strength.

Capricorn also hold lower vibrations. This Full Moon is a time to uncover any of them in your energetic field and shift them as well. Capricorn helps us gain clarity and focus our attention on what matters most. It helps us uncover our life's work and commit to the soul. The lower vibrations of this sign forget the higher meaning of life and instead focus on activities that gain superficial success or power. The lower vibrations of this sign are overly concerned with career gain and advancement, even if it means self-betrayal. The soul is forgotten and its mission is ignored. When we align with the lower vibrations of Capricorn, we become unaligned with our life's work.

If you find yourself becoming more concerned with accumulating wealth, recognition, or unhealthy standards of success, know you have fallen into the low side of Capricorn. Also know that it's ok. Remember, these low sides are impersonal. They can happen to anyone and are universal energies. Simply recognize that these energies have stated to take over, then make a commitment to shift them. Find ways this Full Moon to return home to yourself. What does your heart want? What does your soul want? Acknowledge places in your life where you are simply showing up to be seen or to gain praise or power. Ask yourself what your real motives are for doing something. If they don't align with your soul's values, make a change.

The low side of Capricorn can also cause us to become hyper-focused on work for the all the wrong reasons. This side is the epitome of the workaholic type who spends hours on the computer forgoing basic nourishment like food or self-care. Become aware if you are embodying this side and lean into Cancer's energy to balance it. Give yourself a vacation full of self-care and soul nourishment. Get in touch with how you really feel and ask yourself if you are overworking yourself to avoid these emotions. Allow yourself to feel, and through these feelings gain the wisdom needed to create a life that aligns with your soul and feels good to your heart.

As we shift the lower vibrations of Cancer and Capricorn, we give space for their higher vibrations to integrate in our energy. These signs complement each other and teach us how to achieve a true work-life balance in which we are fulfilled by our life's mission, are guided by our intuition, and give ourselves the self-care needed to replenish the spirit. In working with these energies, we can return home to ourselves as we decide how we want to feel and what kind of life supports these feelings. We also teach ourselves that we can have it all. We can have life filled with love, family, and self-care while still sharing our brilliance with the world through our life's work. Feel the possibility of creating a life full of the highest side of these powerful energies this Full Moon and know it all starts with the willingness to feel.

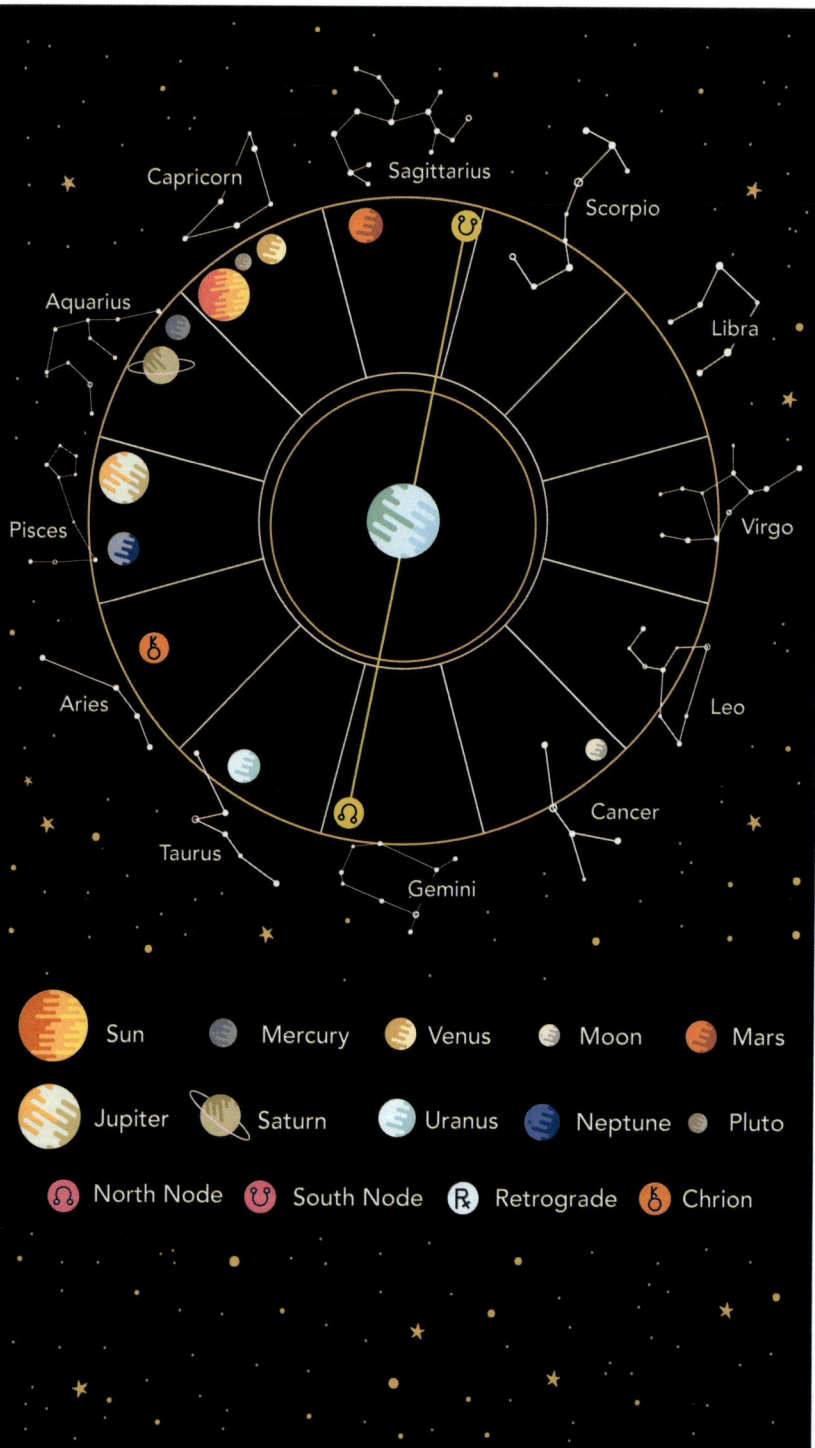

ASPECTS

The Moon and Sun do not exist in the sky alone. There are other cosmic bodies and energies that influence the energy of the Full Moon. On this day the Sun is conjunct Pluto in Capricorn, while the Moon opposes them both. Pluto helps us process the cycles of our lives. This planet rules birth, death, and rebirth. It governs the energy of transformation as we shift from one form to another over our many lifetimes.

Pluto helps us understand everything we endure in this life within the framework of the evolving nature of our energy. Our energy existed before this lifetime and will go on long past it. It is on a course of evolution, attracting events and people to help its journey. What happens this lifetime may resolve something that happened in a past life or may be preparing our energy for the future. Pluto helps us make sense of these ongoing cycles and see them as continued energetic evolution over the context of time.

The influence of Pluto this Full Moon adds to its potential for deep healing. Cancer's energy helps us heal old and new wounds. Through feeling our emotions and processing the events of our lives, we can heal the pains of our hearts. While we may not be able to change the past, we can take steps to make sure we don't suffer because of it. In healing we do not close off a part of ourselves. We open it. We give it room to expand, to breathe and be seen. Healing involves opening and letting our feelings take up the space they deserve. This Full Moon gives us the support to receive what we need to heal.

With the help of Pluto, we can heal through understanding the larger picture of our energy. Feel into what needs healing this Full Moon. Then see it as part of your energetic journey. Know that even your pain helps you grow. It serves an important role in your evolution, even if it was unwanted or feels unnecessary. See how your wounds have shaped you and contributed to this version of yourself. Then love that person. Know you are exactly where you need to be in this moment. While you may not understand the deeper meaning of your wounds just yet, they have helped make who you are today. They have contributed to your power, your strength, and your light.

The Moon also forms a trine aspect with Neptune in Pisces, while the Sun forms a sextile aspect to the planet of dreams. Both of these aspects are harmonious and add to the energy of the Full Moon. Neptune helps us feel our visions and see the future. It heightens our intuition even more on this Full Moon, and inspires us to see past today and into tomorrow.

Neptune reminds us to set time aside to simply be. In that space we allow our dreams to arise. As you move through this Full Moon, pause and do nothing. Stare at a body of water if available, daydream, be open to inspiration and insights. Allow yourself to float away in your mind and take a needed break from your emotional processing. Feel expansive in your energy as you open to new possibilities coming to you from the ethers of existence.

The Sun also forms a trine aspect with the North Node, while the Moon sextiles it. The North and South Lunar Nodes shift signs on January 18, the day after the Full Moon. They are highly active at this time and feed more energy into this day. The North Node reminds us of where we are ultimately heading in this life. It brings up questions of dharma, including our purpose and karmic path. Dharma is a Buddhist term that refers to our duty this lifetime. When we follow our dharma, we uphold the energy and vibration of the Universe. We also free ourselves of some of the suffering of being human.

Over this Full Moon, feel into the combined forces of Capricorn and Cancer as they work with the North Node. Ask yourself what makes you feel good and able to hear your intuition. How does that intuition lead you to your life's work? Finally, how does your life's work raise the vibration of everyone around you?

HOUSESCOPES

The following horoscopes are based on the house that Cancer rules for you. The current Full Moon in Cancer is transiting this house for you and activating it. Houses show us areas of our lives, and they show us where we will feel the effects of this Full Moon most profoundly. You can look up your natal chart at astro-charts.com to find the house ruled for you by Cancer.

Cancer First House: Your very identity is rooted in your emotions. You define yourself by how you feel, along with the ability to take care of yourself. You also define yourself by how you take care of others. With the Moon transiting your first house, it's time for a fresh start. Perhaps this means redefining yourself in some way or reinventing yourself in the eyes of others. Feel into your intuition on this Full Moon to guide you in taking the first steps in this process. Learn to trust yourself now more than ever, especially if you feel lost or unsure of what to do next.

Cancer Second House: You cautiously seek out security, taking your time with decisions around abundance. You focus on building a life full not only of material possessions but also family, friends, and intimate connections. These relationships provide meaning and worth to your life. As the Full Moon activates this house for you, notice areas of your life where you may feel insecure, then ask yourself how you can strengthen your foundation. This may mean having a talk with a trusted friend, asking for what you need, or focusing on self-care. Feel the power of your intuition this Full Moon and know it is your greatest asset.

Cancer Third House: You need to feel nurtured and respected to have honest conversations with yourself and loved ones. You have many feelings to express; in your highest vibration, you do so with clarity and intent. With the Full Moon activating this house for you, be curious about the world around you. Communicate with others, ask questions, and be open to learning something that can help your path of healing. Ask questions of your intuition and patiently wait for the answers, knowing they will arrive.

Cancer Fourth House: The Fourth House is naturally home to Cancer and aligns quite well with this energy. You place great emphasis on the energies that make you feel at home. This includes people close to you, your physical home, and emotions that put you at ease. With the Full Moon activating this house for you, create time to have a conversation with your heart. Feel the center of your soul by simply being. You may also find it helpful to spend time with people who put you in touch with your heart and to feel nurtured by their presence. Focus on your inner self this Full Moon and find your path home.

Cancer Fifth House: Getting in touch with your inner child helps you create and express yourself. You also enjoy activities that bring you back to the joys you experienced as a child and do well with hobbies that align with your younger self. With the Full Moon activating this house for you, feel into what brings you joy—true joy, the kind that brings a smile to the heart. From this place of bliss, feel into your most creative self and allow your intuition to take over in expressing your creativity. Experiment with different creative outlets to share your emotions, especially your joy.

Cancer Sixth House: The Sixth House shows us how we give our gifts to the world. For you, it's important that you feel emotionally ready to share your talents and give to others. You need to find joy in everything you do, from being of service to others or doing mundane activities around the house. With the Full Moon activating this house for you, take a leap of faith and put something out into the world even if it causes you to feel insecure. Align with the power of the Moon to help you overcome any self-doubt and know that you are already good enough.

HOUSESCOPES

Cancer Seventh House: Emotionally secure partnerships are essential for you, and you may choose partners who mirror early childhood bonds. You need to feel nurtured in your relationships and know that you can both give and receive energy. With the Full Moon activating this house for you, reach out to people you feel safe and secure with to help you navigate the many emotions this time brings. Lean on others to help you process, but also know that ultimately the work is yours to do. Support is pivotal for your growth. Be grateful for your team, and let them know how much they mean to you this Moon.

Cancer Eighth House: You are incredibly intuitive and even psychic. You must learn to control your power at a young age and use it for good, not evil. A strong spiritual base is essential for your evolution and energetic survival. If you want to remain in higher energy frequencies, you must develop practices that open up your energetic potential. With the Full Moon activating this house for you, focus on your powers of transformation and regenerate your spirit by transmuting old emotions. Feel your highest compassion and understand both for yourself and others this Full Moon.

Cancer Ninth House: Many people in your life look to you for guidance from an early age. You are a natural teacher and seek knowledge in many forms. You are drawn to spiritual, psychological, and philosophical theories from all over the globe. You may even travel with the intent of gathering them, although it's always important for you to have a home base. With the Full Moon activating this house for you, feel into what you need to release to make space in your energy for new vibrations. Also, feel how you can nurture the part of you that wants to guide others and recognize your power to teach.

Cancer Tenth House: Your life's work is centered around how you care for and nurture yourself. Practices, tools, and routines that you've developed to heal yourself often become the gift you give others. They also become what you are known for, even turning into your public identity. With the Full Moon activating this house for you, feel into what regenerates your soul and feel if it is the right time to give it to the world. This Moon has the power to activate your calling and lead you to your life's mission. Let go of any self-doubt or defeating thoughts and step into your highest frequency as you take on the challenge of raising the vibration of the world.

Cancer Eleventh House: You find nurturance in groups and teams. You need to maintain your identity and emotions within a group, always feeling into your unique identity. Feel into your intuition when it comes to leading others and forming a community. You can be an effective leader when you speak from your heart. With the Full Moon activating this house for you, feel how you are part of something larger than yourself. Also, feel how you can help others—some of whom you may not even know. Allow this Full Moon to open your heart and expand your compassion for all people.

Cancer Twelfth House: You feel at one with the Universe and every being in it. You energetically and emotionally merge with others. Your compassion and nurturing attitude make you a great healer, one with a focus on the higher meaning of life. You are emotionally generous with those around you and seek to teach others the higher philosophies that come naturally to you. With the Full Moon activating this house for you, let go of your old self and feel your infinite potential. Find healing in patience, dedicating time to meditating, sitting with yourself, and observing your emotions. Trust in your intuition, your powers, and your ability to restore yourself and others.

CANCER LUNAR FLOW

The Full Moon in Cancer is a time to settle into ourselves and allow our bodies to unravel. We often hold suppressed emotions in our muscles and connective tissues, which contributes to our feelings of emotional attachment. To allow our emotions to flow freely, we need to release our bodies and the energy they hold. The following sequence is a yin sequence, which relies on longer holds than a typical yoga practice. In holding postures, we can release into the pose fully and allow the body to unwind completely. In each pose, focus on your breath and use it to keep your mind clear as your body lets go of tension. Also, have support ready in the form of a blanket, bolster, or blocks. When we have physical or mental support, we are more likely to release and let go of tension.

To begin, come to a seated posture, sitting on a blanket or a bolster. Have a timer handy and set it for 3 minutes. During these first minutes, focus solely on your breath. On the inhale, count to 4; on exhale, count back down from 4. Continue this counting for the remaining time. This is the pace of the breath for the entire practice. Use the numbers to help focus your mind and keep it from wandering away from the present moment.

Baddha Konasana // Cobbler's Pose: 5 minutes

Bring your feet together with your knees out to either side for Baddha Konasana. Prop your hips up on a blanket if needed. You can also place blocks under your knees for support. Gently fold over your legs and allow your back and neck to relax. Once you are in a yin pose, hold it and breathe. There is less emphasis on alignment in these types of poses versus vinyasa or hatha postures. Continue to count up to 4 and back down from 4 as you breathe, allowing your body to unwind. If you are met with resistance in any area, try sending your breath to that area and asking it gently to open up.

Janu Sirsasana // One-Legged Forward Fold: 3 minutes each side

Extend your legs out long on the mat. Sit on top of a blanket and take your right foot to the inside of your left leg. Fold over your front leg. You can have your blocks stacked by your leg to support your forehead as you fold. Allow your spine to round and your head to be heavy. Relax your leg and let your foot be soft. Breathe here for 3 minutes, allowing your hamstrings to open, sending your breath into this area. Slowly switch sides, giving yourself and your body time to unwind in the transition.

CANCER LUNAR FLOW

Ardha Apanasana (Supported) // One-Legged Knee-to-Chest Pose: 3 minutes each side

Lie on your back and have your bolster or block nearby. Place it under your hips, propping yourself up into a slight backbend. Hug your right knee into your chest and stretch your left leg long. Feel an opening in your left hip as you breathe here for 3 minutes. Let go of tension in your shoulders and neck. On each exhale, feel your body sink into the floor a bit more. After 3 minutes, slowly switch sides.

Setu Bandhasana (Supported) // Bridge Pose: 3 to 5 minutes

While on your back, bend your knees and have your feet hips width apart. Have your blocks nearby. On inhale, lift your hips into Bridge Pose. Place two blocks under your hips, feeling your entire body supported. Allow yourself to rest entirely on the blocks. Have your arms by your sides and place slight pressure on your triceps, pressing the floor away to open your chest. Release the pressure and focus solely on your breath for 3 to 5 minutes. On each exhale, let go of tension in your neck and shoulders. Once the time is complete, slowly remove the blocks and set your back down one vertebra at a time, pausing at the bottom.

Supported Fish Pose: 5 minutes

You can use either a bolster or two blocks for this pose. If using a bolster, place it lengthwise on your mat and lie over it, with it supporting your spine and head. If using two blocks, which is a deeper pose, place one block on the tallest height for your head and the other block lengthwise, so it fits in between your shoulder blades. Lying on both blocks or the bolster, either place your legs into Baddha Konasana or have them straight on the mat. Place your palms upward in a receptive position and feel your entire body relax. Allow your heart and chest to expand, and feel into the vulnerability of this position. Know you are safe and supported. Allow yourself to fully receive the gifts of this pose and the new energy flooding into your being.

Supine Twist: 3 minutes each side

Remain on your back. Hug your left knee into your chest once again and twist to the right side. You can place your bolster or block under this knee to give support to your twist. Stretch your right arm out to the side, but keep your neck neutral. Fill your low back with your breath as you breathe, releasing more into the twist on each exhale. After 3 minutes, slowly come up and switch sides.

Savasana: 5 minutes

Stretch your legs out long on the mat. Have your palms facing upward in a receptive position. Allow your entire weight to be supported by the floor beneath you as you rest. Let go of counting the breath and breathe naturally, observing the quiet flow of inhale and exhale.

FULL MOON MEDITATION

The following meditation is a version of mindfulness meditation to help you regulate and balance your emotions. Take your time with this one, and do it only for as long as you feel comfortable. If emotions become too intense at any point, know you can always rest in the breath.

Begin in a comfortable seated position or lying down, fully supporting your body. Close your eyes and first breathe into your belly. Expand your abdomen with each breath, filling up like a balloon. Exhale completely, deflating your lungs and stomach. Breathe like this for 1 minute, calming your entire nervous system. When you feel ready, notice what emotions are present in your body. This can be anything from irritation to joy, sadness, or even contentment. Acknowledge any feelings that are present in your field and label them, giving them definition. Just observe what they are for a moment, then scan your body, feeling for physical sensations associated with a particular emotion.

Locate the space where you hold your emotions and feel the sensations that are associated with them. This may be tightness, heaviness, or any other sensation. Without trying to change anything, observe which bodily sensations arise when you experience certain emotions. Bring your awareness to the strongest sensation in your body. Create an outline, or container, around that sensation, isolating it from the rest of your body. Become fully aware that this sensation does not make up your entire being but instead occupies only a part of your energetic and bodily field. Once you have the emotion and corresponding sensation contained, breathe into the container, filling it with energy and love. Continue to breathe into this space and notice what new sensations arise. Do this without trying to change what already exists within you. Simply witness your feelings. Allow new sensations to develop and be felt. This may bring up fear or other feelings, or it may make you feel lighter in your body. Anything that occurs is exactly the right thing for this moment. Continue breathing into your container, giving your body and energy time to process the emotion. Continue holding space for your emotions, letting them move freely, shift, and change. Know that they will pass and that every sensation we feel is temporary, even if it feels like it isn't. Through bringing awareness and compassion to your emotions, you give them the chance to release from your field.

Continue breathing into your container for 5 minutes, or longer if you like. Stay fully present with yourself through the process. Do not rush yourself or force a release before it is ready. Also, do not overthink your emotions. Just stay present with them and give them space to breathe. When you're finished with the feeling, dissolve the container and allow that part of you to integrate back into the rest of your field. Bring your attention back to your breath in your belly. Continue to practice abdominal breathing for another minute, recentering yourself.

CIRCLE SET UP

The following are rituals you can practice this Full Moon, along with the practices in the workbook. You can do any or all of them. It's best to practice within forty-eight hours of the Full Moon exact to receive the complete magic of this lunar cycle phase.

Hold a Full Moon Circle

Celebrate this first Full Moon of 2022 with people you love. Cancer connects us with our families—soul or biological. Call in the people who feel like home to you and hold a circle to honor your connection under the Full Moon. If you are feeling like being with yourself today, know you can also hold a circle just for you. Follow your intuition in deciding who to practice with; some Moons will feel more private, while others will feel more festive.

Choose a space that feels grounded, supportive, and nurturing. Your circle can be inside or outside. It can contain as many or as few objects as you like. Use your intuition when setting up a circle—especially when placing objects. Below are suggestions on how to set up and hold a Full Moon circle.

• Begin by opening yourself to guidance from yourself and the Universe by saying, "I am open to guidance."

• Set the perimeter of your circle with crystals and candles. Use crystals for Cancer and Capricorn. These include Rose Quartz, Selenite, Moonstone, and Sodalite for Cancer, and Garnet, Bloodstone, Fluorite, and Hematite for Capricorn.

• Set the center of the circle with a large crystal, crystal grid, or candle. If using a crystal grid, create it in a circular or spiral shape with a sphere in the center to represent the Water element.

• Once the perimeter is set, visualize a white light encasing the circle, providing both protection and purification.

• Cleanse the circle with a dried herb bundle. Lavender is an excellent herb for Cancer. You can use it as a bundle or loose in a bowl. Fan the smoke from the herb around the circle, starting in the most easterly point and moving clockwise.

• Before you or your guests sit in the circle, cleanse them and yourself from head to toe. Once you have all entered the circle, pause for a moment to let the energy settle before you begin.

• Begin with each member introducing themself. Talk about the astrological energy of the day and how it is affecting each one of you. Share and learn from each other about your unique experiences with this Full Moon.

• Practice the yoga and meditation in this book.

• Complete the practices in this book after discussing the content.

• Talk more about your experiences with the practices and do the card-reading practice.

• Close the circle by giving gratitude to everyone who chooses to honor the Full Moon with you. Give thanks both to the elements for supporting you and the energy of the Universe for guiding you along the way.

CIRCLE SET UP

Moon Bath

You can include a Moon bathing ritual alongside your circle or alone. If you are practicing it within the circle, include it during the meditation practice. You can also include a second session of Moon bathing after you've completed the practices as a way to process the knowledge you learned and integrate it into your energetic field.

Moon bathing is a simple practice. Much like sunbathing, it allows you to absorb the energy and light of the Sun reflected from the Moon. It can create a sense of calm within you and help you feel connected to your intuition as the fluctuations of your mind settle.

• Find a space outside that allows you to lie directly in the Moon's light.

• Set out a blanket or lie directly on the Earth.

• You can practice this with clothes on or off. You can even practice it in a bathing suit.

• Lie under the Moon with the palms of your hands up in a receptive position.

• Spend 20 to 60 minutes under the Moon. You can listen to a meditation or meditate on your own.

• Absorb the light of the Moon and allow it to soothe your soul.

• Complete your Moon bath by thanking the Moon for her light.

• Bonus practice: Place four pieces of Rose Quartz around you to amplify the energy of the Moon: one above your head, one below your feet, and one to each side.

• Bonus practice: Take a cleansing bath afterward, especially if you need to warm. Fill your bath tub with Epsom salts, dried lavender, Rose Quartz crystals, and a few drops of chamomile essential oil. These elements soothe the soul and provide relaxation to your body and mind. As you enjoy your bath, state three things you are releasing from your energy and dunk your third eye (center of your forehead) in the water with each statement.

CARD READING

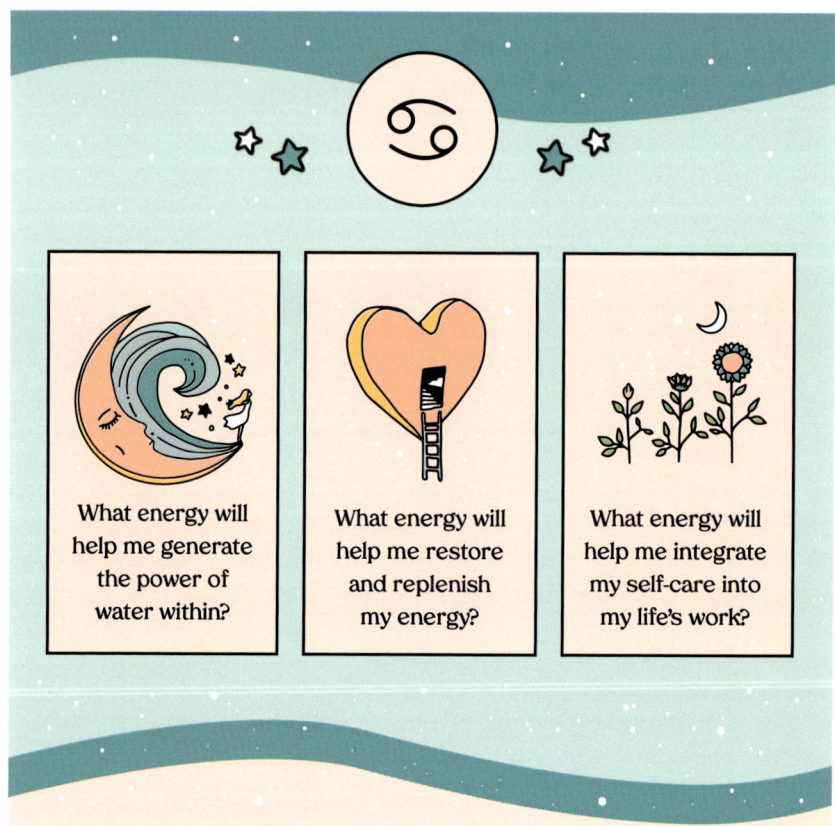

Reading Cards is a beautiful way to access your intuition and tap into your, and the Universe's, higher wisdom. Anyone can pull cards, as long as you are willing to receive the information they provide. You need no prior experience, or training, just an open and clear mind.

You may use any cards you like for this practice, including but not limited to: Tarot Cards, Animal Medicine Cards, Oracle Cards or any Affirmation Cards. You also can pull cards from a few decks to gain different perspectives. If you are new to card pulling, try to ask only one deck the same question, as asking different decks the same question can become quite confusing. Below are some general guidelines on how to pull cards. Please improvise as needed and above anything else, listen to your intuition.

Clear Your Mind
A settled, grounded mind is essential for pulling cards. The last thing you want is random thoughts running around when you are trying to receive clear answers from yourself. Practice the breath work and meditation in this workbook to prepare and settle your mind. You may also clear your mind using sound frequencies through singing bowls. These can either be crystal or metal bowls. Play the bowl, or bowls, for about 3-5 minutes to help rid your mind of external noise as you focus on the harmony of the sound.

CARD READING

Pick Your Deck
There are many different decks out there. You can choose as many as you like. Know, though, that they each provide you a different energy or medicine. Tarot Cards are the most popular and should be used carefully. Although very useful, Tarot cards can give the wrong impression if you interpret them harshly. Animal Medicine cards offer different types of messages from the animal realm which can help align with the spirit of nature. These cards give you the medicine you need to apply to your situation or question. Affirmation cards provide you with guidance in the form of words or phrases. When reading these cards, it is best to meditate on what the affirmation means for you. It is also helpful to repeat the affirmation a few times and see how it makes you feel. There are many other cards you can experiment with, like Goddess Cards, Angel Cards, and so on. The important thing to remember with any card is that they each have different angles and sides. There are often a few interpretations of the same card.

Shuffle
Shuffle the cards the easiest way for you. Some cards are smaller and can be shuffled like a regular deck of playing cards, while others with take some effort. If all else fails, spread them out on the floor in front of you then regather them. Keep a clear mind while shuffling. You can also repeat " I am open to receiving guidance and intuition." Refrain from asking your questions until the next step.

Cancer Card Questions
You are free to ask the deck any questions you need answers to on this Full Moon. The following questions are meant to help you harness the energy of Cancer through the cards to clarify some of these energies in your mind. This is a three-part card reading, where you'll ask the deck three questions. Before beginning, spread your freshly shuffled cards in a wide arc in front of you. Use your left middle finger to choose the card, first waving your hand slowly over the cards. You'll feel a magnetic pull, or slight tingle, in your fingertip when you hover over the right card. Chose one card at a time, taking a moment to breathe in between questions. Keep the cards flipped over until you pull all three.

What energy will help me generate the power of water within?

What energy will help me restore and replenish my energy?

What energy will help me integrate my self-care into my life's work?

Take Them In
Once you have your cards, flip them over. Before looking up their meaning, sit with them for a moment and allow them to speak to you. Intuit your own meaning and interpretation of the card. What is the card trying to tell you? What are you trying to tell yourself? After a few moments with the cards, look up their meaning. Sit with that information, merging it with your intuitive meaning of the cards.

As with everything, enjoy this process. Do not worry if you are doing it right or wrong. Just follow your intuition, and trust the journey. Accept the cards you are dealt and use their energy wisely to help guide you when you need it the most.

20

LIKE THE OCEAN,
SOMEDAYS YOU'LL MOVE
SLOWLY AND SOFTLY.

WHILE OTHER DAYS
YOU'LL FEEL THE NEED
TO ROAR AND CRASH.

BOTH ARE BEAUTIFUL.

———

SPIRIT DAUGHTER

CANCER PRACTICES

The energy of this Cancer Full Moon teaches us first to honor our emotions. From our emotions flows our intuition. As we find our inner compass, it then leads us to what feels like home, including people, projects, places, and our life's work. This Moon is a time to sit with your feelings, process them, and learn from them. Everything starts with feeling. As your emotions heighten this day, know they are here to teach you and help you grow.

Before you explore your emotions, it's important to understand what you need in order to feel supported. Cancer is the great mother. It teaches us to receive what we need from ourselves and others. As you begin the journey of this Full Moon, ask for what you need from both yourself and others. Asking for our needs can be challenging. You first need to identify them in yourself, then have the courage to share them with others. Know that you deserve to have your needs met. You are worthy of receiving support, love, and encouragement this Full Moon and always.

1. What makes you feel supported and held by yourself, the Universe, and others?

CANCER PRACTICES

_____

_____

_____

_____

_____

_____

_____

_____

_____

2. What is something you need to help you process your emotions? Is this something someone else needs to give you? Or can you give it to yourself?

_____

_____

_____

_____

_____

_____

_____

_____

_____

_____

_____

_____

_____

CANCER PRACTICES

Know that the Moon is showing up for you today, just as you are showing up for yourself. Simply by doing the work in this book, you are giving yourself support and love. Full Moon practices in themselves are an act of self-care. Give yourself love and appreciation, and return to this love if you feel overwhelmed by any emotions that surface.

Finish this statement: "I feel ..." Write unrestricted, not holding back.

_____

_____

_____

_____

_____

_____

_____

_____

_____

_____

_____

_____

_____

_____

_____

_____

_____

_____

_____

_____

_____

CANCER PRACTICES

3. What do your emotions help you understand?

_____
_____
_____
_____
_____
_____
_____
_____
_____
_____
_____
_____
_____
_____
_____
_____
_____
_____
_____
_____
_____
_____
_____
_____
_____

CANCER PRACTICES

4. What wisdom do they provide?

CANCER PRACTICES

As you unravel some of your emotions this Full Moon, decide how you want to feel. Create your home frequency—the vibration you can return to no matter what occurs in your life. Your home frequency is a baseline for your vibration. You may spend days in other vibrations or emotions, but ultimately your energy always knows where to return to after you define your home frequency. It takes work and commitment to cultivate this frequency, but after some time it will become the energy of your life.

5. What do you want to be your home frequency? Gratitude? Love? Contentment? How do you want to feel each day?

CANCER PRACTICES

6. What practices, rituals, or life changes support this frequency?

_____

_____

_____

_____

_____

_____

_____

_____

_____

_____

_____

_____

_____

_____

_____

_____

_____

_____

_____

_____

_____

_____

_____

_____

_____

CANCER PRACTICES

Deciding and cultivating your home frequency can also help you understand your life's work and how to balance it with your self-care. Ultimately, you want to pursue a mission this lifetime that feels good to your soul. It should support your home frequency and help maintain it. If something is disturbing to your home frequency or distracts you from how you want to feel, that it is not aligned with your soul. When you are in soul alignment, your work and purpose allow you to tend to yourself and nourish your energy. Your life's work can feel nurturing and not depleting. It can feel good and allow you periods of self-care that replenish you.

7. How does your life's work support the way you want to feel? If you haven't found your life's work, what would support your home frequency?

_____

_____

_____

_____

_____

_____

_____

_____

_____

_____

_____

_____

_____

_____

_____

_____

_____

CANCER PRACTICES

8. What lets you know that your energy is depleted and it's time for self-care? Do you become overly emotional? Numb?

_____

_____

_____

_____

_____

_____

_____

_____

_____

_____

_____

_____

_____

_____

_____

_____

_____

_____

_____

_____

_____

_____

_____

CANCER PRACTICES

9. In your ideal world, how often do you need self-care each week to feel centered and focused in your body and mind?

CANCER PRACTICES

Life also doesn't have to feel like a struggle. There can be an ease to life if you align with your feelings, intuition, and soul. Getting to that place can be challenging, but know that it is possible to have it all. It is possible to enjoy a life full of joy, purpose, and contentment. It all starts with believing it is possible, then taking steps to create it in reality.

How can you have it all without feeling like any of it is a struggle? This is a larger vision that can take years to manifest, but as we venture into 2022, try to expand your perceptions to include a life full of everything that brings you joy without having to work so hard to obtain it. Envision a balanced life in which your work restores you, your relationships fulfill you, and your time alone helps you align with your intuition and move forward in your life with ease and grace.

The main message of this Full Moon is about your intuition. It is where you will find all the answers to the questions of this Moon and to the questions of life. Honor your intuition today and every day. If you feel inspired or gain a flash of brilliance, follow it. Your intuition knows so much more than you can imagine. It is connected to the many energies, and if it is pointing you in a certain direction, trust it.

10. What does your intuition feel like?

_____

_____

_____

_____

_____

_____

_____

_____

_____

_____

_____

_____

_____

_____

CANCER PRACTICES

---

11. What helps you trust and follow it?

CANCER PRACTICES

Additional Space for Journaling

AFFIRMATIONS

Take a moment and imagine what it feels like to be completely nourished. Imagine your energy is full, you are alive with inspiration, and your heart is healed. Write down some words that describe this feeling. Do you feel whole, held, or ready to greet the day? What does your frequency feel like? Do you vibrate with the energy of gratitude, love, or compassion? Write down as many words as you need to describe this feeling of being nourished in your soul.

_____

_____

_____

_____

_____

_____

_____

_____

Now create three to five affirmations to take with you into the new year that use the words listed above. Write powerful "I am" statements that help you tell the Universe how you want to feel each day and the energy you are ready to receive.

_____

_____

_____

_____

_____

_____

_____

_____

_____

_____